KALEIDOSCOPE

THE SUPREME COURT

by
Suzanne LeVert

BENCHMARK BOOKS

MARSHALL CAVENDISH
NEW YORK

Benchmark Books
Marshall Cavendish Corporation
99 White Plains Road
Tarrytown, NY 10591-9001
www.marshallcavendish.com

Library of Congress Cataloging-in-Publication Data

LeVert, Suzanne.
The Supreme Court / by Suzanne LeVert
         p.cm. – (Kaleidoscope)
Includes bibliographical references and index.
ISBN 0-7614-1453-3
1. United States. Supreme Court—Juvenile literature. 2. Judicial power—United States—Juvenile Literature.
[1. United States. Supreme Court. 2. Courts. 3. Judicial power.] I. Title. II. Kaleidoscope (Tarrytown, N.Y.)

KF8742.Z9 L38 2002
347.73'26—dc21

                              2001007572

Photo Research by Anne Burns Images

Cover Photo: 2001 Jay Mallin

The photographs in this book are used by permission and through the courtesy of: Jay Mallin: p. title page, 5, 33; The Granger Collection, NY: p. 6, 9, 22; Corbis: p. 25, 29, 10, 17; Reuters NewMedia Inc.: 26, 42 Bettman; 34 Franklin McMahon, 38 Wally McNamee; Archive Photos: p. 13, 41; CNP Liaison Photos: p. 14 Mike Theiler/Getty Images; 30 Bill Wisser; Hulton Archive: p.18, New York Times Co./George Tames; 37 New York Times/D.Gortson; North Wind Pictures: p. 21

Printed in Italy

6 5 4 3 2 1

CONTENTS

EQUAL PROTECTION

"Equal Justice Under Law" is the motto inscribed over the entrance to the Supreme Court Building in Washington, D.C. It states the primary purpose and goal of the highest court in the land—to make certain that all people receive equal protection under the laws of the United States of America.

Completed in 1935, the Supreme Court Building was designed to reflect the dignity of the Court and its importance as an equal branch of the federal government. This marble statue, called the Guardian or Authority of Law, is a seated male figure holding a tablet of law backed by a sheathed sword, representing enforcement of principles through law.

5

In a carefully balanced document called the *Constitution*, our founding fathers created the U.S. government in 1787. The Constitution divides the government into three branches. The *executive branch*, made up of the president of the United States and his cabinet, enforces the laws. The *legislative branch*, consisting of Congress, enacts the laws. The *judicial branch*, or the courts, interprets those laws. As the nation's highest court, the Supreme Court makes sure that those laws remain true to the Constitution.

The founding fathers created a strong judicial branch when they wrote the United States Constitution, which established the United States government.

INTERPRETING THE CONSTITUTION

Almost all cases decided by the Supreme Court involve "federal questions." Federal questions are issues that relate to the meaning of the Constitution, and the interpretation of federal laws. The Constitution provides all citizens with certain rights. If a law, an act of government, or a decision by another court of law denies those rights to a citizen, the Supreme Court can declare that law or decision unconstitutional. Rarely, the Supreme Court decides cases that involve disputes between two states or between one state and the federal government.

Article III of the United States Constitution outlines the makeup and responsibilities of the judicial branch of the government. Here is the first page of the Constitution as prepared and signed into law on September 17, 1789.

We the People

of the United States, in order to form a more perfect Union, establish Justice, insure domestic Tranquility, provide for the common defence, promote the general Welfare, and secure the Blessings of Liberty to ourselves and our Posterity, do ordain and establish this Constitution for the United States of America.

Article. I.

Section. 1. All legislative Powers herein granted shall be vested in a Congress of the United States, which shall consist of a Senate and House of Representatives.

Section. 2. The House of Representatives shall be composed of Members chosen every second Year by the People of the several States, and the Electors in each State shall have the Qualifications requisite for Electors of the most numerous Branch of the State Legislature.

No Person shall be a Representative who shall not have attained to the Age of twenty five Years, and been seven Years a Citizen of the United States, and who shall not, when elected, be an Inhabitant of that State in which he shall be chosen.

Representatives and direct Taxes shall be apportioned among the several States which may be included within this Union, according to their respective Numbers, which shall be determined by adding to the whole Number of free Persons, including those bound to Service for a Term of Years, and excluding Indians not taxed, three fifths of all other Persons. The actual Enumeration shall be made within three Years after the first Meeting of the Congress of the United States, and within every subsequent Term of ten Years, in such Manner as they shall by Law direct. The Number of Representatives shall not exceed one for every thirty Thousand, but each State shall have at Least one Representative; and until such enumeration shall be made, the State of New Hampshire shall be entitled to chuse three, Massachusetts eight, Rhode Island and Providence Plantations one, Connecticut five, New York six, New Jersey four, Pennsylvania eight, Delaware one, Maryland six, Virginia ten, North Carolina five, South Carolina five, and Georgia three.

When vacancies happen in the Representation from any State, the Executive Authority thereof shall issue Writs of Election to fill such Vacancies.

The House of Representatives shall chuse their Speaker and other Officers; and shall have the sole Power of Impeachment.

Section. 3. The Senate of the United States shall be composed of two Senators from each State, chosen by the Legislature thereof, for six Years; and each Senator shall have one Vote.

Immediately after they shall be assembled in Consequence of the first Election, they shall be divided as equally as may be into three Classes. The Seats of the Senators of the first Class shall be vacated at the Expiration of the second Year, of the second Class at the Expiration of the fourth Year, and of the third Class at the Expiration of the sixth Year, so that one third may be chosen every second Year; and if Vacancies happen by Resignation, or otherwise, during the Recess of the Legislature of any State, the Executive thereof may make temporary Appointments until the next Meeting of the Legislature, which shall then fill such Vacancies.

No Person shall be a Senator who shall not have attained to the Age of thirty Years, and been nine Years a Citizen of the United States, and who shall not, when elected, be an Inhabitant of that State for which he shall be chosen.

The Vice President of the United States shall be President of the Senate, but shall have no Vote, unless they be equally divided.

The Senate shall chuse their other Officers, and also a President pro tempore, in the Absence of the Vice President, or when he shall exercise the Office of President of the United States.

The Senate shall have the sole Power to try all Impeachments. When sitting for that Purpose, they shall be on Oath or Affirmation. When the President of the United States is tried, the Chief Justice shall preside: And no Person shall be convicted without the Concurrence of two thirds of the Members present.

Judgment in Cases of Impeachment shall not extend further than to removal from Office, and disqualification to hold and enjoy any Office of honor, Trust or Profit under the United States: but the Party convicted shall nevertheless be liable and subject to Indictment, Trial, Judgment and Punishment, according to Law.

Section. 4. The Times, Places and Manner of holding Elections for Senators and Representatives, shall be prescribed in each State by the Legislature thereof; but the Congress may at any time by Law make or alter such Regulations, except as to the Places of chusing Senators.

The Congress shall assemble at least once in every Year, and such Meeting shall be on the first Monday in December, unless they shall by Law appoint a different Day.

Section. 5. Each House shall be the Judge of the Elections, Returns and Qualifications of its own Members, and a Majority of each shall constitute a Quorum to do Business; but a smaller Number may adjourn from day to day, and may be authorized to compel the Attendance of absent Members, in such Manner, and under such Penalties as each House may provide.

Each House may determine the Rules of its Proceedings, punish its Members for disorderly Behaviour, and, with the Concurrence of two thirds, expel a Member.

Each House shall keep a Journal of its Proceedings, and from time to time publish the same, excepting such Parts as may in their Judgment require Secrecy; and the Yeas and Nays of the Members of either House on any question shall, at the Desire of one fifth of those Present, be entered on the Journal.

Neither House, during the Session of Congress, shall, without the Consent of the other, adjourn for more than three days, nor to any other Place than that in which the two Houses shall be sitting.

Section. 6. The Senators and Representatives shall receive a Compensation for their Services, to be ascertained by Law, and paid out of the Treasury of the United States. They shall in all Cases, except Treason, Felony and Breach of the Peace, be privileged from Arrest during their Attendance at the Session of their respective Houses, and in going to and returning from the same; and for any Speech or Debate in either House, they shall not be questioned in any other Place.

No Senator or Representative shall, during the Time for which he was elected, be appointed to any civil Office under the Authority of the United States, which shall have been created, or the Emoluments whereof shall have been encreased during such time; and no Person holding any Office under the United States, shall be a Member of either House during his Continuance in Office.

Section. 7. All Bills for raising Revenue shall originate in the House of Representatives; but the Senate may propose or concur with Amendments as on other Bills.

Every Bill which shall have passed the House of Representatives and the Senate, shall, before it become a Law, be presented to the President of the

A case begins when two parties have a disagreement that they bring before a court of law. The case is named after the two parties. For example, if George Smith sues the United States government because he believes the government has wronged him, the case would be called *Smith v. United States.* (The v stands for *versus*, which is Latin for "against.")

Legal conflicts between two parties are resolved in courts of law. Courts are presided over by judges, who rule on issues of law.

A case usually goes before the Supreme Court when someone loses a legal case in a lower federal or state supreme court and asks the Supreme Court to review the decision. First, the Court determines whether the case involves a dispute between states or between a state and the federal government—which is very rare—or a federal question, which forms the basis of most Supreme Court cases. If the case does involve a federal question, the Court may choose to hear the facts of the case and then rule on whether or not the person's constitutional rights were preserved. Called *judicial review*, this process allows the Court to examine the laws of the land to make sure they conform to the requirements of the Constitution.

Cases that come before the highest court of the land, the Supreme Court, usually involve questions about whether a state or federal law properly protects the rights of citizens under the Constitution.

THE HIGHEST COURT IN THE LAND

The founding fathers believed that creating a national legal system was very important. In fact, the first bill passed by the United States Senate was the Judiciary Act of 1789. It gave the president power to nominate new Supreme Court justices, and it provided for a federal and a state court system. One of the most controversial provisions of the act, Section 25, granted the Supreme Court the right to hear states' high court appeals when the decisions involved questions of the constitutionality of state or federal laws.

The attorney general is the head of the judicial branch. In 2000, President George W. Bush nominated John Ashcroft to the position, and the Senate later confirmed him. Attorney General Ashcroft helps administrate the federal courts of the United States.

The structure of the federal court system is like a pyramid. At the bottom of the pyramid are the ninety-four U.S. district courts, which are the first courts to decide federal cases. If the losing party in a trial in a district court is dissatisfied with the decision, he or she can appeal the case to one of the thirteen U.S. Courts of Appeals, which make up the next level of the pyramid. At the top of the pyramid is the Supreme Court.

In this state court, Judge Nikki Taylor hears the case of Florida voters who feel that their absentee ballots were not counted correctly during the highly contested 2000 presidential election.

Each of the nine Supreme Court justices has one vote, and the majority rules. When a majority of the Supreme Court votes on a constitutional issue, their judgment is final. The decision can be altered only if Congress amends the Constitution. However, the Court has occasionally reversed one of its own earlier decisions.

United States Supreme Court decisions usually involve questions about how federal laws affect individual rights.

THE SUPREME COURT THROUGH TIME

The Supreme Court first met on February 2, 1790, in New York City, which was then the nation's capital. Chief Justice John Jay and the associate justices worked for two years to define the Court's powers and duties. In 1792, they heard and decided their first case. For the first ten years, however, the Court was the weakest branch of the government, mostly because the Constitution did not define its powers very well.

Prior to becoming chief justice, John Jay served as secretary of foreign affairs. Following his term on the Court, he served two terms as governor of New York.

1829

But all that changed in 1801, when President John Adams appointed John Marshall of Virginia to be the fourth chief justice. In 1803, under Marshall's direction, the Court defined its role in the case called *Marbury v. Madison*. In that case, the Supreme Court established its power to interpret the U.S. Constitution and to determine the constitutionality of laws passed by Congress and state legislatures. Marshall went on to serve as chief justice for thirty-four years.

John Marshall, who served as chief justice from 1801 until his death in 1835, wrote 519 out of the 1,000 decisions made during his tenure. His decisions helped strengthen the Court. Here, he is pictured taking the oath of office.

LANDMARK DECISIONS

Throughout its history, the Supreme Court's decisions have had profound effects on the nation and the lives of its citizens. The Court sometimes must decide issues between the national government and the individual states. During the Civil War (1861–1865), for instance, the Southern states tried to leave the Union and form a separate country. When the war was over, the losing Southern states returned to the Union.

The issue of slavery divided the nation in the late nineteenth century. In this political cartoon, a Union general battles a seven-headed serpent symbolizing the South.

GENERAL SCOTT.

25

THE HERCULES OF THE UNION,
SLAYING THE GREAT DRAGON OF SECESSION.

One of the Supreme Court's most important jobs is to rule on issues of civil rights—the rights individual citizens have to live in society as free and equal people under the Constitution. In the 1954 decision *Brown v. Board of Education*, for instance, the Court ruled that having separate schools for black students and white students—a practice called *segregation*—was unconstitutional. Another important civil rights issue decided by the Court concerned the rights of people who have been arrested in connection with a crime. In the 1966 case *Miranda v. Arizona*, the Court ruled that anyone arrested for a crime must be told of his or her constitutional right to remain silent and to have legal representation, or a lawyer, present during all legal proceedings against him or her.

In 1954, the Supreme Court ruled that laws that separated white and black students in different schools were unconstitutional. The process of integration—bringing white and black students together in the same facilities—began.

THE SUPREME COURT IN ACTION

Today, nine justices—or judges—sit on the Supreme Court, but that hasn't always been the case. Before settling at nine in 1869, the number of Supreme Court justices changed six times. Throughout its entire history, the Supreme Court has had sixteen chief justices and ninety-seven associate justices.

The president of the United States nominates Supreme Court justices. Two-thirds of the Senate must approve the nomination for the candidate to become a justice. Justices serve until they retire, die, or are *impeached*. On average, justices have served for about fifteen years.

Thurgood Marshall became the first African-American Supreme Court justice after President Lyndon B. Johnson appointed him in 1967. He retired from the Court in 1991 and died in 1993.

ENDURING COURT TRADITIONS

When the Court is in session, the marshal of the Court announces the entrance of the justices into the courtroom at ten o'clock in the morning and raps a desk with a gavel. At the sound of the gavel, those present rise and remain standing until the justices are seated. Since at least 1800, it has been traditional for justices to wear black robes while in court. The chief justice wears a black robe with a salmon-colored collar. The nine justices are seated according to seniority, or the length of time they have served on the court. The chief

Here, a judge of a lower court peers over the bench with his gavel in hand.

justice occupies the center chair, the senior associate sits to the right, the second senior to his left, and so on, alternating right and left by seniority.

The term of the Supreme Court begins on the first Monday in October. Court sessions usually continue until late June or early July. The term is divided between "sittings," when the justices hear cases and deliver their rulings, and "recesses," when they consider the business before the court and write opinions.

Justice Ruth Bader Ginsburg is seen walking down the steps of the Supreme Court Building with Chief Justice William Rehnquist.

The Court considers about twenty-five cases at each sitting. Since most of the cases involve a review of another court's decision, there is no jury and there are no witnesses to hear. For each case, the Court examines a record of what occurred in the lower court, along with *briefs*—written arguments—from both sides. Each side's attorney may present his or her case in an oral argument in front of the justices for thirty minutes. In recess, the justices work on their opinions and consider requests to hear new cases.

The Supreme Court receives requests to hear about seven thousand cases per term. Of that number, the Court hears about one hundred oral arguments and renders about eighty to ninety formal written opinions.

FILLING A VACANCY

When a justice dies or retires from the Supreme Court, the president of the United States selects a nominee—usually a judge from a lower court—and then the Senate considers his or her qualifications. After holding hearings, the Senate votes to confirm or deny the appointment. If more senators vote for confirmation than against it, the nominee becomes a Supreme Court justice.

Nominated by President Ronald Reagan and confirmed by the Senate, Sandra Day O'Connor became the first female Supreme Court justice on September 25, 1981.

The process of selecting a new justice can be quite political, because the Court makes decisions that affect the lives of individuals and the nation as a whole. In choosing a new justice, the president and the U.S. Senate consider not only the nominee's experience, but also his or her opinions about certain issues.

In 1987, the Senate failed to approve Robert Bork because of his strong opinions against abortion and affirmative action.

THE COURT TODAY

Today, William Rehnquist is the chief justice. He was appointed to the Court in 1972 by President Richard Nixon and became chief justice in 1986. There are two women associate justices, Sandra Day O'Connor and Ruth Bader Ginsburg, appointed by Bill Clinton in 1993. They are the first women to sit on the Supreme Court. Associate justices John Paul Stevens, Clarence Thomas, Antonin Scalia, Anthony Kennedy, David Souter, and Stephen Breyer join them. The two eldest members, Justice Stevens, and Chief Justice Rehnquist, are expected to retire by 2005. If they do, the president of the United States will nominate justices to take their

Judicial Branch the branch of government responsible for interpreting the laws of the nation, headed by the Supreme Court

Judicial Review the power of the Supreme Court to review the constitutionality of acts passed by Congress or actions by the president

Legislative Branch the branch of government responsible for creating the laws of the nation, made up of the two houses of Congress, the Senate and the House of Representatives

Segregation the separation or isolation of a race, class, or ethnic group by discriminatory means

FIND OUT MORE

BOOKS

Goldish, Meish. *Our Supreme Court.* Brookfield, CT: Millbrook Press, 1994.

Patrick, John J. *The Supreme Court of the United States: A Student Companion.* New York: Oxford University Children's Books, 2001.

Quiri, Patricia Ryon. *The Supreme Court.* New York: Children's Press, 1998.

WEBSITES

If you want to see copies of the original Constitution, Bill of Rights, and other documents of national importance, this is the site to check out:
National Archives
www.nara.gov

This website offers links to many congressional offices and also allows you to search to find out information about individual bills and issues:
Thomas: Legislative Information on the Internet
http://thomas.loc.gov/home/legbranch/legbranch.html

Read about important constitutional law cases, past and present, as well as find out information about current Supreme Court justices:
Selected Supreme Court Decisions
http://supct.law.cornell.edu

AUTHOR'S BIO

Suzanne LeVert is the author of nearly a dozen books for young readers on a host of different topics, including biographies of former governor of Louisiana Huey Long and author Edgar Allan Poe. Most recently, she wrote four books in Benchmark Books' Kaleidoscope series on the human body, *The Brain, The Heart, The Lungs,* and *Bones and Muscles.*

INDEX

Page numbers for illustrations are in **boldface.**